ACTIVATE OR STAGNATE:

Strategies for your personal and business life to get and stay fired up for success.

Gregory Griffith

Gotham Books

30 N Gould St.
Ste. 20820, Sheridan, WY 82801
https://gothambooksinc.com/

Phone: 1 (307) 464-7800

Published by Gotham Books (November 9, 2023)

ISBN: 979-8-88775-617-2 (H)
ISBN: 979-8-88775-464-2 (P)
ISBN: 979-8-88775-465-9 (E)

Table of Contents

The Inspirations & The GG Factors

I dedicate this book…

To God for the insight and innate vision to bring my thoughts and inspirations into written expression.

To my Mother for all the times I couldn't feed, clothe, or even think for myself. You made the decisions that gave me the foundations for success.

Above all things Mother, thank you for taking me to church! I love you immensely!

To you Miriam "Maru" Griffith for your relentless unconditional love. I can't thank you enough for just believing in me.

I love you more than you'll ever know!

Foreword

Someone once said motivational speakers are useless because they get you all worked up and once they leave, so does the motivation.

What I have come to discover about life is that it is a daily process of renewal. Think about it for a moment. Who stops bathing because they bathed one time and the effects of the bath wears off? It's absurd to think people would stop doing something that is so essential to their health and well-being.

The same is true of personal empowerment and motivation. It is a daily commitment to reinvent yourself and to stand firm in your commitments 100% of the time. Inspirational speakers like and Greg Griffith and me, play a significant role in reminding, reconnecting, refocusing, and reenergizing people who seem to forget the value of daily personal development. Out of a great love for people and the fulfillment of our dreams, we live in a commitment for people's lives working everyday!

That's why Greg has prepared this very simple but powerful tool for you. *Activate or Stagnate* walks you through 30 days of introspection, self-discovery, and self-motivation. Each day offers you a powerful thought that you can use to center and focus upon as you build a day of committed action.

You may read this book in sequence or you may choose to read it out of sequence. The key is to "use the book." Should you find a page especially inspiring, enlarge it, copy it and post it on your mirror or someplace where you will see it regularly to remind you to stay focused.

Every day you will receive new insights as you appropriate and activate each of these powerful statements into your life. Let this book be the catalyst for you to establish your own routine of quiet reflection, personal introspection, and a daily commitment to living your best life.

Greg Griffith is a motivational speaker and author committed to sharing his story of personal transformation through these unique life lessons. Work with them everyday and see yourself break through stagnation and move on to your personal motivation.

Rev. Dr. Kevin Kitrell Ross

Author, inspirational speaker, Creator of the Designer Life Coaching System and Senior Minister of Unity of Sacramento

www.kevinrossspeaks.com   www.unityofsacramento.com

Acknowledgements

The inspiration to write this book has come from so many of my life experiences that began many years ago. I know it's impossible to remember and acknowledge everyone whose presence has impacted my life.

I've been blessed to meet some incredible people from my childhood to this present day.
I deeply thank…

Every teacher and coach who took the time to help me expand my mind and build my confidence

Rev. Dr. Kevin Kitrell Ross for the empowering sessions as my coach and spiritual advisor I not only looked forward to our sessions but
To our prayer time.

Rev. Mary Tumpkin and the Universal Truth Center for keeping me grounded in spirit through this entire process. I love you Mary!

Dr Tina Dupree and the entire Professional Speakers Network for the forum to grow.

Gregory and Jonathan, my two sons, and my granddaughter, Alyssa. I live and die for you three!

Cheryl and Anita for giving me two stable, healthy and intelligent gifts from God

My brother Nelson for his love and guidance: Thank you for my trumpet.

Thank you for my first bass guitar. Thank you for riding me around town on the back of your bicycle. I love you more than you'll ever know!

Ruby and Linda my sisters for giving me nothing but love and
support.
Ruby, you were my first lead singer when I could barely hold my
bass on my shoulder
You were the wind beneath all of our wings even at 12 years old.
Thank you!
I love you both beyond measure.

Gail because you know I love you like a sister. We shared too
much with Linda and Ruby!

Pansy. I miss you more than words can say. I'm sure we'll meet
again in spirit.

My editor and new friend for life; Zandra Faulks. I know you're
God sent!

All my Exceptional students and faculty,
Especially Dr. Sharon Shaulis at Flanagan High in Pembroke
Pines, Florida
I'll always remember you in my humble beginnings as a speaker
A very special thank you to Mr. Tim Mogilka and the Flanagan
TV
Production team
Thank you, Dr Patrick and Commander Stephen Nesthus
All of your support was priceless!

To Essex. You'll always be my other brother. Thank you for
everything!

All the musicians and singers who paved the way for me as a
band leader
You believed I could get the job done. I learned so much from all
of you.
Thank you, James JT Taylor, Israel Charles, Rachel Brown!
Rachel, I know you could have taken many other offers

You believed in me against all odds. It's made all the difference!

Kathleen Brady and Melanie McCutcheon for believing my message needed to be heard by some wonderful kids in other Broward County Schools.

Thank you very much Robert Downey and Tera Tedesco Faso for your support to get my message to our Broward County Public Schools students and staff.

To the principal of West Broward High School, Mr. Brad Fatout and the ESE and TV Production Departments at West Broward High. You gave me a platform as a practitioner of education to empower and inspire our youth to successfully transition to post school adult living.

What People Are Saying About Gregory Griffith and Activate or Stagnate!

As a colleague I've known Gregory for five years, and admired his efforts, but a year ago I was fortunate to see his work up close as he offered his assistance to my football team and me. Our team showed great potential but seemed to lack the spark it needed to achieve the status it desired. Gregory addressed the team before one of its games and offered the players an opportunity for excellence. And though one might be hard pressed to attribute our team's subsequent success, which included three straight wins to finish the best season in the school history to a single factor, I am convinced that Greg's short speech ignited our players just as his efforts have inspired his students. Greg Griffith's Personal Empowerment Recognition Program (PERP) has enriched many lives and I am indebted to him for sharing his skills with our team.

Gregory's unique approach motivates students to excel by combining artistry with enthusiasm and convincing young people to realize themselves as vital players in their own development. For years he has provided at risk and disadvantaged children with the spark, which has emboldened them to achieve academic success and take pride in their accomplishments. Gregory's approaches are many and varied and may include fiery oratory song and dance, but his compassion is unmistakable. His message never veers from the spirits of the students he serves.

--- Dan Marguriet, Head Football Coach

Extremely well-articulate, witty, and provocative, Griffith provides his readers with a fast track to activate their inner excellence. Both a mentor in-person and in writing, Gregory Griffith is always available to give tough truths and help others commit to self-improvement. It's a powerhouse read you won't forget, with palpable positive impacts that can benefit anyone.

--- Roxana Alberti
West Broward High School
Post Graduate Alternative for Secondary Students

Activate or Stagnate/30 Days to A New You is an inspiration for people of all ages that serves to empower mind, body and spirit. Gregory is an outstanding motivational speaker and creator of the Personal Empowerment Recognition Program (PERP).

--- Sheri Wilson, Speech Pathologist M.S

Worldwide success can be found in *Activate or Stagnate/30 Days to A New You.* My students and I have found these principles to be on point to motivate teens and adults to doing the right thing for the whole (emotional, physical, spiritual) person.

--- Chandra Powell, Business Professionals of America,
Business Ed. Teacher

Activate or Stagnate is a tool to build character and integrity in our youth. The strategies empower the reader to become and remain focused on high achievement for success at transition.

--- Dr. Sharon Shaulis, High School Principal

Mr. Griffith's PERP is a class act. PERP encourages students to think before they act. I highly recommend *Activate or Stagnate* to implement the PERP lifestyle strategies to motivate students and athletes.

--- Kelvin P. Lee, High School Principal

Gregory Griffith is a lively, high-spirited role model for the youth of today. *Activate or Stagnate/30 Days to A New You* enlightens and inspires people to believe in themselves and to make the right life style choices.

--- Cyndy Porco, Art Teacher,
Department Chair Person, Teacher of the Year

Gregory Griffith's *Activate or Stagnate* is a body or work that captivates and inspires the reader just as Greg's performances helps students achieve personal growth. It's a must read for youth and adults seeking to take their lives to the next level.

--- Joan Ash, Retired Personnel Administrator

Gregory Griffith's Activate or Stagnate reflects a commitment to success. It provides powerful, inspirational strategies for growth in mind, body and spirit.

--- Georgia Foster, Toastmaster Club President

I have known Gregory for over 10 years as a professional educator. Greg is a master motivator and positive force in the lives of countless students as well as colleagues. His deep commitment to helping others, especially those with special needs, is admirable. Those individuals blessed to have been in Greg's universe, have been inspired, motivated and fortunate. I can count myself as one of the fortunate! Thank you.

--- Mr. Rodney Sell, ESE Department Head
West Broward High School

Mr. Griffith inspires both students and adults to achieve greatness. His enthusiastic approach to learning and life greets all who are lucky enough to be in his presence. Mr. Griffith embodies the idea of people evolving to become better versions of themselves. With each interaction, Mr. Griffith plants the seeds for growth that can be watered for a lifetime of successes.

--- Marnie Weissmark, ESE Specialist
West Broward High School

While reading your book, my mind, body and soul received so many positive vibes. I feel rejuvenated and refreshed. I WILL SHARE THESE LIFESTYLE STRATEGIES FOR PERSONAL GROWTH WITH MY CHURCH GROUP.

Our time together at WeBro has left such a remarkable impact on my career. I witnessed your patience, kindness and authentic love for your students. Being a black male in our profession, is a rarity. And you personified Black excellence as an educator. Your personality exudes happiness, dedication, and strength. You are a true inspiration. I will miss our smiles and your endless compliments. Many mornings, I looked forward to seeing you because of your infectious optimism and the way you tackled each day with a positive outlook.

Thank you for sharing your book and beliefs with me.

Blessings always.

--- Mrs. Michelle M. Bellamy, West Broward High
Professional School Counselor

Greg Griffith is a speaker and colleague that impressed me beyond expectations. I have personal experience of working with Greg, he will go beyond just being a speaker. He does more than just speak for his clients. His content, engagement enthusiasm is very inspiring. Invite him to speak for your event and you will certainly be rewarded with a great presentation.

--- Keynote Speaker
Dr. Robert Lemon

Gregory Griffith is a talented and dynamic educator that takes all of his student's individual needs in to account when providing them the tools for success. He has the ability to not only motivate his students, but colleagues as well. His words resonate and stay with you. Activate or Stagnate 30 Days to a New You is an engaging read that is not only thought provoking but will inspire you to excel in all areas of your life.

--- Roberto Diaz, LMHC, LPC, NCC
Psychotherapist and Broward County
Public Schools Family Counselor

"Activate or Stagnate" is a thought-provoking and insightful self-help book that offers practical advice on how to achieve personal growth in all areas of life. It can lead you to examine you physical, mental and spiritual wellness with a goal of being a winner in life!

--- Mishele Difede
School Counseling Director
West Broward High School

Quote for the book:
"Be the light that helps others see."
- Anonymous

Introduction

In September 1992, I was fresh out of graduate school from Barry University in Miami Florida. I'd just been hired to work as an Exceptional Student Education (ESE) teacher at Coconut Creek High School. Although I had worked as a substitute teacher for some time, this was my first fulltime teaching position. It was also the first full time job I'd taken since I left college in 1976. Life for me was quite different. I was a new daddy and my son Jonathan and his mother Anita were the reason I went to graduate school to become a teacher. After fifteen years of traveling and playing night clubs as a professional entertainer, I made a decision to slow down and be there for my family. I've always felt guilty of not being able to spend more time with Gregory, Jr., my older son. His mother moved to North Carolina and I only got to see him on holidays and in the summer from the time he was in high school through college.

I was excited, full of enthusiasm and ready to be the best ESE teacher I could be. I got a quick wake up call to all the demands of my job right away. Imagine your first year in the classroom starting without a classroom of your own. I had six classes that I had to push a cart with my materials on and hustle to get to each class and be ready to get kids to learn who didn't want to come to school. Even when they showed up, my first and most difficult task as an ESE teacher was to get them motivated, focused and eager to learn.

ESE students have learning disabilities that make it difficult for them to process, retain and recall information. My classes were larger than usual for ESE students and along with the learning disabilities, most of my kids were emotionally handicapped (EH). EH kids can be very moody and sometimes extremely violent. Now that you've got the picture in your mind, just imagine the job I had facilitating our ESE curriculum and praying for some level of recall and retention.

I knew immediately I had to be innovative and develop non- traditional methods of teaching to create an environment for learning that made the kids want to show up and exhibit the proper behavior for learning. I developed a motivational program derived from writing to my students on a daily basis. Every day when they entered the classroom I would

1

have a motivational journal of inspirational information I would have them copy in a composition book. The inspirations became a part of me and there began the etiology of my Personal Empowerment Recognition Program (PERP). Our great discussions and open dialogues help me create lasting student teacher relationships with kids who opened their hearts to me and began to believe they were unique and have a contribution to make to society regardless of the extent of their learning disability. PERP helped each student establish basic foundations for physical, mental and spiritual development to become successful at transitioning to post secondary school living. PERP gave each student an opportunity to discover their purpose, their passion for life.

I've compiled 30 of my inspirational strategies from hundreds of the PERP sessions I've had over my 30 years as an ESE teacher to empower you and your family to take charge of your life and your future.

I suggest a timeline of 30 days as a simple but powerful window of time to allow you to set up a PERP from the simple questions I'd like you to answer about your physical, mental and spiritual development. When you've answered the questions, you'll have a quick assessment of where you are from a physical, mental and spiritual perspective. This is not a quick fix. PERP is a lifestyle management tool. In 30 days, I personally guarantee that your life will be improved and different if you honestly answer the questions and get fired up and focused about your life.

Read each inspiration and get ready to take charge of
your life NOW.
Remember NOW means No Other Way! Good luck! God
Bless you and your family!

Personal Empowerment Recognition Program Questionnaire (PERP)

Physically

- Are you exhibiting your optimum physical appearance (OPA)?
- Are you disciplined about exercise?
- What are you fueling your tank with?
- Are you aware of the consequences of ignoring the physical?

Mentally

- Are your goals set to achieve greatness with the skills you possess?
- Do you feel you're ready to meet the mental challenge?
- Will fear of failure be the winner?
- Are you a peak performer?
- Are you honestly trying to expand mentally?

Spiritually

- Are you in touch with the source?
- Have you discovered where the real power is?
- Do you know how important creativity is to your success?
- Are you being unique or trying to blend in?
- Are you utilizing your inner perspective to grow from every external challenge?

The Inspirations
&
The GG Factors

Activate or Stagnate!

In each of us is an infinite amount of
Energy to reach our maximum potential.

Not realizing it is like having an *engine running* but
never putting the gear shift in *drive*.

When you awake, you have to *activate the energy*
within by giving more to simply be more.

You've got to *activate* your thoughts to drive on the
highway to success or you'll stagnate from
procrastination. It's your choice.

Activate or Stagnate!
Nothing happens if you don't take action!
Don't procrastinate to the point of stagnation!
Plan your strategy. Stay consistent, FIRED UP and
FOCUSED!

The GG Factor
Activate or Stagnate

In life we have a way of making excuses for why we don't seek to reach our maximum potential. How many times have you had an idea that required a little more of your time and focus to get results?

Instead of working to bring your idea to fruition, you just comfortably transform all your pre-existing obligations into insurmountable obstacles to your growth. You just remained in the comfort zone of your life from day to day.

I know because I was a victim of the same circumstance. I worked my job and came home to a routine regimen until I realized that life offered me more than the comfort zone of an 8 to 5 job that allowed me to make some one else rich and far more secure than I'd ever be.

I'm sure you have a daily routine from which you can't deviate without creating a conflict with your family, a girl or boy friend, a manager or just your neighbor next door. But sometimes you just have to take a serious look at where you are and determine if it's where you really want to be in life from the physical, mental and spiritual perspectives. The foundations for success in life—to obtain and maintain a balanced lifestyle-- lie within those three areas. I asked you to answer the questions from a mind, body and spirit perspective only to bring awareness to the forefront in your life.

Procrastination is the major reason for stagnation of the mind, body and spirit. Don't be a victim of circumstance like I was. I started to eat healthier foods, exercise on a regular basis, set challenging realistic goals to advance my position in life and I consistently seek to grow from the spiritual perspective and from my belief that faith works wonders!

Take the next 30 days and let each of the inspirational
Strategies empower you to take your life to the next level.
It's time pull your life in drive!

ACTIVATE OR STAGNATE!

My notes on activate or stagnate:

My personal plan:

**GET ACTIVATED!
STAY FIRED UP IN
MIND, BODY AND
SPIRIT!
IF I DID IT, YOU
CAN TOO!**

If I did it, you
can too!

**Barry University
Commencement Day Ceremony
1992. Gregory received his
Masters Degree in Exceptional
Student Education.**

Do You Have a Foundation?

How quickly do we forget that the tree is supported by its roots.

If you start with a good foundation, you will be prepared to handle life's complex situations.

The balance we need can only be found using the right combination of *physical, mental, and spiritual foundations.*

Build your life like the roots of an old tree; it's the beginning of your own personal life history.

The GG Factor
Foundations

Foundation is defined as an idea or system for lifestyle development that becomes the ground work for success. You must establish a balanced foundation to accommodate the continuum of life's changes. You see, we all must go through to get to this place of balance. There are no exceptions to the rule.

I have two sons, Gregory and Jonathan. Both were given foundations for success at very early ages in very different environments and under different parental supervision. Gregory was shifted between parents early and didn't get the attention from which his younger brother was able to benefit simply because the foundation was established for Jonathan after I became cognizant of how important balanced foundations are for success, not only to me but to my entire family.

Granted, both my sons are very stable, healthy and intelligent. Gregory had more of a struggle than Jonathan only because of the delay in establishing the foundations correctly. If more parents remember that the tree is supported by its roots, we'll have a more balanced successful society---physically, mentally and spiritually.

The imbalance that a great many deal with in society has a chaotic effect on us all. As a high school teacher and a coach for 31 years, I see the blatant apathy among those responsible for establishing the foundations for success. It is quite evident in a society that tolerates a 65% obesity rate, lack of creative finesse, and a moral and spiritual decline that has manifested as a large prison population, lowered numbers of college graduates and a spiritual struggle in the midst of a high tech society.

Don't be an apathetic victim.

Establish the
FOUNDATIONS!

My notes on establishing foundations:

My personal plan:

My Family Foundation.
Mother Essie Mae Griffith

My personal family foundation

"WE MUST CONSISTENTLY SEEK SPIRITUAL GROWTH"

I read Psalm 91 everyday.

"He who dwells in the secret place of the most high shall abide under the shadow of the almighty".
Don't leave home without it.

Me and
Rev. Larry Roundtree
Senior Minister at Mount Zion
Baptist Church Tampa, Fl.

My spiritual mentor:
Dr. Rev. Marcus
Davidson
Senior Minister
New Mount Olive
Baptist Church
Ft. Lauderdale, Fl.

Mount Zion Baptist Church

Gregory was baptized at
Mount Zion Baptist Church
in 4th grade.

**My mom Essie Mae Griffith with me
and my sister Linda Baker as kids.**

**My Parents: Essie Mae Griffith
& Willam Hammond**

Graduation Day from Florida A&M University with my Mother, Essie Mae Griffith

A Mother's Day visit to Mount Zion Baptist Church Tampa, Fl.

Greg's childhood home, Tampa Fl.

17

HAPPY NEW YOU!!!

Yesterday. Last month. Last year.
All are part of our personal history books. It's good to take a mental look back at them, but please do not get hooked on the events of the past.

Nothing you can do now will change that which simply has passed. It's a new day! You now have the chance to travel life's roads a different way.

To start again is a beautiful part of the next beat of your heart. Get the rhythm of life right---now!

Set new goals.

Don't let fear stop your chance to dance to the rhythm of life.

HAPPY NEW YOU!!!

The GG Factor
Happy New You

I vividly remember the spring of 1990. I was experiencing a very, very happy new year. My son Jonathan was born on February 27,1990. His mother had conceived against all the odds. Jonathan was a miracle baby. I was working as a full time musician six nights a week and as a substitute teacher during the day to support my family.

I'd been performing for about seven months at a nightclub in Ft. Lauderdale, Florida when I got a reminder of the true instability of the entertainment business. I arrived at work as usual and was asked to speak to the club's manager on break. He informed me that the club was happy with our services but had an opportunity to get an act that was available for only a few weeks.

We were supposed to be hired by my agent to start another club the next week and return to play at the current club when the road band completed their show. It didn't happen! I was now faced with a dilemma. I have a newborn baby, no job and my wife is on maternity leave!! This was not a new scenario regarding the job change. The big difference was I now had a baby to feed, a mortgage and two cars to pay for. I was also my band's leader and manager, which meant I also had the financial livelihood of six other musicians on my shoulders! Boy was it time for me to get the rhythm of life right.

The next day I decided to set new goals for my family and my future. I continued to work as a musician but I made a commitment to go back to school to have a more secure financial base. I applied for graduate school and found that one class at Barry University in Miami, would cost me $500. I applied for financial aid and went to school on Saturdays from 8 am to 5 pm for one year. My last show on Friday nights didn't finish until 3 am.

Could you just imagine how I felt on Saturday mornings? But you see I made the commitment to not look back at my past. I took a look but didn't get hooked. I had to travel life's road a new way. I graduated one year later and became a fulltime high school teacher and coach.

What's your dilemma you're faced with right now? Do the obstacles seemed insurmountable? Are you going to let the fear monster stay on your back and stop you from reassessing your life for the new you that starts right now! NOW is a powerful three-letter word. I use it as an acronym - <u>N</u>o <u>O</u>ther <u>W</u>ay. NOW! Maybe my little story will get you fired up and focused NOW for the new you, to take charge of your life and reach for the next level.

Life is always about the next level! As they say at Adidas:

"IMPOSSIBLE IS NOTHING!"

My notes on happy new you:

My personal plan:

Reverend Frank Kennedy;
Gregory & Miriam Griffith wedding day.

My Honeymoon cruise 2019.

My 60th birthday celebration.
A blessed moment!

HIT THE HOMERUN!

You are the *umpire* in the game of life!

You can go to bat as often as you like until you hit a homerun!

Strikeouts are never failures. Each one is just a learning experience that prepares you to hit the homerun!

Never give up on your dream!

Keep going to bat until you

HIT THE HOMERUN!

The GG Factor
Hit the Homerun

Life will throw quite a few curve balls at you. Just don't be afraid to strike back. Against all the odds you've been able to stay in the game and keep going to bat. Sooner or later you'll make the connection to hit the big one!

Do you think the great Willie Mays hit a homerun the first time he went to bat? We only know about the homeruns. You wonder, how many times did Willie strike out before he hit the first homerun?

DO YOU REALLY THINK THAT WILLIE MAYS COULD HAVE HIT A HOMERUN IF HE DIDN'T KEEP GOING TO BAT?

Think about the story of Sarah Reinertsen. She had her left leg amputated at birth due to a rare birth defect. At the age of seven she wanted to play soccer. Her coach took one look and made her just practice kicking the soccer ball against a wall.

You'd think that Sarah would quit! Never give it another chance. She got a physical therapist to teach her how to run with a prosthetic leg and has never looked back!

Sarah forgot soccer but went on to become a world-class sprinter, half and full marathoner for ladies with a prosthesis. She went on to train and compete in triathlons in college. She's presently training to be the first female amputee to finish an iron man triathlon.

Sarah actually wanted to quit several times in her career before going on to smash the world record for female above-the-knee amputees. She wanted to hit the homerun to success as a female prosthetic athlete.

Sarah never gave up on her dream. You see, Sarah realized it's always closer than it seems.

You got to think like Sarah! Keep going to bat!!

Hit the homerun!

My notes on hitting the homerun:

My personal plan:

Oneness

This you must affirm:

I am one with love, peace and understanding from my constant innate source.

Wherever I am, the source is.

My past has no power over me.

My true reality lies in the here and now.

Nothing or no one can keep me from realizing this truth.

The source and I are one, and I can never be separated from it!

The GG Factor
Oneness

T he four "I" effect that you must never forget: The source is *innate, intrinsic, inherent* and *inborn*.

Faith can't work if you do not internalize it. The source is as close as the air that you breath if you'll just believe!

My mother took me to church from the age of five until I left home for college at seventeen. My foundation for dealing with anything in life is grounded on the principle of faith from the source. I don't know how many times in my life I've been faced with circumstances that just seemed to be out of my control. The only hope I had of seeing a favorable outcome was to just turn within and accept that my internal dialogue with my source would guide me in the right direction.

To this day as an adult, my faith has taken me through the storms of my life. As a marathon runner I have to reach deep inside when the wall comes up after the 20th mile. It becomes mind over matter. The source has to be there for me. At the age of 50 I ran the New York City marathon. It was my 9th marathon. My training regimen was somewhat stagnated by injury with less than two months to race day. I started to swim and run less to allow my leg time to heal. When I did start to run again I experienced the same problem with my leg muscles collapsing.

This time I decided to reach within and find the strength from my source to keep my focus and complete the run. My strategy changed to slow down run ten minutes and walk three minutes and just continue to have faith that I could complete the run. I did! The very same thing happen to me thirty minutes into the NYC marathon. I didn't get my best time but I did complete the marathon in 4:40. For the record my marathon personal record is 3:29.

The source!
You can't leave home without it!!

My notes on oneness:

My personal plan:

God is! I Am!

We must connect with our innate SOURCE.
I'm so grateful to my Mom for taking us to
church as a kid. She kept us grounded in
GOD.

GENIUS!

When the UNIQUE you opens the door for the creative you to come shining through, something great happens!! The GENIUS comes out to play for a day!

Your personal contribution represents the intrinsic, the inherent, unique genius that's innate in you.

Imagination is an incredible tool to use 24 hours a day, 7 days a week, 365 days a year!

The genius is working even when you're sleeping.

Remember, time is like money.

Don't waste it! Spend it wisely Discover the GENIUS!

The GG Factor
Genius

How many times have you had an idea that appeared to be a great opportunity to become an entrepreneur? How often would you say very quickly, "oh no, not me! I just don't think that I can."?

It's in those very moments of creative bliss that we accept or reject the genius at the door of life. How many times are you going to say "if I could have maybe I would have been…" Every time you procrastinate about the possibility of succeeding or failing, you've only fed another negative thought to stagnate your glory. Have you let the innate power to be all that you've dreamed of just die?

Maybe it's time for a creative resurrection!! Come on! Let the genius come out to play! I know that typically we only associate genius with high intelligence, but please don't confuse genius with a high IQ.

I read a short story about the greatness that singer, songwriter, Lionel Richie manifested in less than an hour for one of his most successful songs. "Easy" was written on a tour bus in 30 minutes. You see you don't know when the genius wants to come out and play. Just be a good sport and get in the game of life when it's your turn to play.

Have you really got the statistics on how many millionaires are just focused, hard working individuals with a vision to recognize when the unique genius is ready to play? You'd be very surprised! Ask Sam Walton, the great genius behind Wal-Mart. The genius inside asked him to come and play discount store owner. The rest is history. Boy, did he come to play!

My notes on genius:

My personal plan:

Growth Potential

Just as a tadpole grows to become a frog, and an acorn becomes a tree, so should you be able to realize your full growth potential.

You see, we're all part of a WONDERFUL DIVINE plan that allows each of us to reach OUR maximum potential hand in hand.

The only difference between you and the tadpole is your ability to plant the seeds for the maximum growth potential that only you can feed.

The GG Factor
Growth Potential

Your ideas are just like the tadpole and the acorn. They're full of all the right ingredients to reach fruition from the source. You see, you've got to get up everyday and feed the idea with your relentless energy.

I remember when I was given my trumpet from my older and only brother, Nelson. He said something very simple but powerful to me at the age of 12. You must practice everyday to get better. No practice! Stagnation!

Frustration!

Well as a 12-year-old I had my long moments of frustration from procrastination. But let me tell you this, when I started to practice everyday, I got results. I began to play all my scales, my armature strengthened. I established the foundations for success as a musician. I went on to make my middle school band and played first trumpet. I went to the same high school my brother attended, Middleton High. He's a retired teacher. I played trumpet in the band because I remained fired up and focused. I continued to feed the idea that I could be a good trumpet player. I graduated from high school and I had the ultimate challenge of making the Florida A&M University Marching Band! I couldn't let my brother down. He also was in that band. I would watch him come home and march in the big homecoming parades and I envisioned the day I'd be there too! Well, I made the band! After a rigorous training regimen and several challenging auditions I was chosen from among some of the best musicians, as one of 200 players who tried out.

I'll never forget the feeling of wearing the uniform and coming home for homecoming feeling like a winner. I planted the seed. The rest was left up to me and the source. Isn't it time for you to plant some seeds? Maybe you've started to get a degree or high school diploma after many years of procrastination and stagnation.

Maybe there's a book you'd like to complete. Maybe there's that great idea for a business that you've just stop feeding. I could go on and on about the infinite possibilities that could be waiting from something as simple as a focused, committed seed to see the dream become reality. Oh yes, indeed! It's never too late to plant a seed.

My notes on growth potential:

My personal plan:

My humble beginnings   **My fourth grade shot**

**My first job was as a paper boy at
age 10 with the Florida Sentinel.**

New Beginnings

New beginnings are sometimes the best thing
That could happen to us.

Change gives us the chance to start again.

Remember you always have a choice, but choices still
Have consequences.

If you do nothing, nothing will change.

Doing something opens the door to new and
Unlimited opportunities.

Don't let the "fear" of change lead to "stagnation!"
Believe in yourself no matter what others say!

The unique you will shine through.

The GG Factor
New Beginnings

When our comfort zones are threatened, we tend to obscure the possibilities that change will bring. All that matters is *what if I fail or what if I can't maintain my basic level of living?*

Security versus freedom and peace of mind becomes the primary issue when we consider a career change or a divorce. A positive attitude is one of your most important weapons against the fear of change. When your attitude is right the universe answers your call with the same level of energy that you give to it.

I remember reading the true story from the book, "Attitude Is Everything" by Keith Harrell. Keith was a great All American high school and college basketball player. His attitude about life was always extremely positive and Keith had his goals set to become an NBA first round draft pick right until the day the NBA draft took place and Keith wasn't drafted. His attitude toward life took a full reversal.

Keith became very pessimistic about his life to the point that he had obscured all the great possibilities his college degree offered him even if he didn't become a professional athlete. It wasn't until someone saw him painting houses in Alaska and recognized him for all that he was beyond just a basketball player that Keith took the right attitude with change and became a very successful salesman for IBM.

You see Keith was so set in his comfort zone with sports that his fear of failure to do anything else was dominant and nothing else seemed to matter or exist as an alternative in his life to be happy. "What a difference it made when Keith decided to activate his attitude in the right direction instead of stagnating his life with a negative, pessimistic attitude."

A new beginning was just waiting!!!

My notes on new beginnings:

My personal plan:

The Contribution

You're here to make your contribution.

Know that your existence in this time and place isn't just a coincidence.

For this reason, enjoy the moment, maximize the opportunity and never regret anything or anyone.

Life is just too short to have a perception that is blurred by negative thoughts or negative people.

Know that there's only good in your life. Absolute good.

It's time to find your passion, your purpose in life.

Make the contribution to the universe that only you could make.

The GG Factor
The Contribution

What one thing you would do in life if you knew you couldn't fail? If you can answer this question without a shadow of doubt, then you've discovered your passion and purpose for your contribution to life. If you cannot answer this question, then now is the time to explore the possibilities.

You know it's never too late to take an assessment of all the pros and cons of your life. If you've been in and out of jobs and relationships, stop to think what was the best part of any of the jobs or people you've spent any consistent length of time with. Sometimes you just can't see the forest for the trees.

Opportunities knock at the door of life and we're so busy with what appears to be the place we ought to be--our comfort zones---until typically something goes wrong.

Activate or stagnate your opportunities in life with optimum awareness and a positive attitude to give to the universe what you're looking for and the contribution will naturally begin. I love to perform and speak. I love to teach and coach. I've found that my contributions are always going to be associated with giving back to people and humanity in the form of information and multi entertainment services. That's why I've written this book of inspirations. It's your time to assess and make your personal contribution.

Please don't forget to make sure in the process of making the contribution you are empowered, excited and very, very, enthusiastic!

42

My notes on contribution:

My personal plan:

West Broward High Prom 2023
West Broward High Principal,
Brad Fatout and his wife Dawn
Gregory Griffith and his wife Miriam

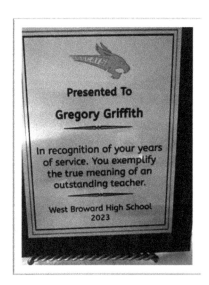

Broward County Public Schools
Retirement 2023

MY FIRST KEYNOTE SPEECH

Gregory Griffith

Marathon Finisher Medals

**Timeline finisher medals.
New York Marathon finisher for my 50th birthday, 2004.**

**Greg's PR is 3 hrs. and 29 mins.
Jacksonville, Fl. Marathon**

Leave your legacy.
It's your unique life
history!

LIFE IS A MARATHON!
IT'S NOT THE
DESTINATION. IT'S
THE JOURNEY ALONG
THE WAY. THOSE
ACCOMPLISHED
GOALS ALONG THE
WAY ARE LIKE
FINISHING ONE MILE
AT A TIME IN A 26
MILE MARATHON!
JUST GO THE
DISTANCE! NEVER
EVER QUIT RUNNING
YOUR RACE! JUST GET
ACTIVATED AND STAY
FIRED UP FOR
SUCCESS!

**West Broward High Exceptional
Student Education Autism Awareness**

**West Broward High ESE
Autism Awareness Day.**

**My last class as a
ESE teacher at
West Broward
High in 2023.**

Empowerment

Empowerment is a personal, constant obligation unique to each of us.

Personal Empowerment is the one thing in life that cannot be avoided.

No empowerment, no qualifications, no growth. No growth is a slow road to stagnation. Don't be a victim of circumstance just afraid to take a chance in life.

Fear is a very powerful form of stagnation.

You must keep the engine in drive and strive for the big prize: SUCCESS.

Quitting simply is not an option if you have a real dream and a vision.

The GG Factor
Empowerment

Martin Luther King, Shirley Chisholm, Jesse Jackson, Ray Charles, Helen Keller, Maya Angelo, Lance Armstrong, Colin Powell, Oprah Winfrey, Magic Johnson, Allen Iverson, Doug Williams, Harriet Tubman, Donnie McClurkin, Robert Schuller, Jackie Robinson, Muhammad Ali, Nelson Mandela…all have faced what appeared to be insurmountable obstacles in their lives, but each had something far stronger than the obstacles, a will to win!

Empowered individuals just intend to win. Peace of mind, optimum health, happy relationships and prosperous ventures are all by-products of the empowerment process to success in life. Start to make the pertinent accommodations and lifestyle assimilations to reach equilibrium. Discover your passion, your true purpose in life through the personal empowerment process.

As Chief Executive Officer of PERP, my mission is to empower individuals to utilize the strategies I've presented here. I hope that you are ready to "ACTIVATE OR STAGNATE". It's your LIFE!!!

My notes on empowerment:

My personal plan:

Keynote shot from Harvard International Academy in Hollywood, Fl.

HARVARD INTERNATIONAL ACADEMY

Gregory Griffith; Miriam Griffith; Ingrid Mason, Principal, CEO; Rodnet Mason, Principal, CEO

ENTHUSIASM!

Nothing could be more gratifying than the thrill of enthusiasm. It's just a time to feel free.

Enthusiasm ignites feelings of sheer delight to this place of spiritual heights!

WOW! Oh how we wish life was always sunny days, bright smiles and laughter in the hearts of all.

For every young mind that hadn't been blemished by life's hard falls, there is an unconditional answer to enthusiasm's call.

There is no fear factor to obscure the thoughts, just thoughts of having a good time, a good life!

Winner takes all---be it big or small.

How many enthusiastic moments have you had lately?

The GG Factor
Enthusiasm

S ometimes we have to take a chill pill on life. Taking anything too seriously too long will lead us down a road to the stress zone. Of course we should keep the focus to see the light at the end, but you got to know when to say enough is enough my friend.

We're all guilty of all work and no play to the point of forgetting about the sun that comes with each day. In September 2000 I went to the hospital with extreme chest pains early one morning when I could barely walk back to my classroom after a fire drill. I spent four days in the hospital being monitored, and given stress tests and every other test associated with heart failure to ensure I was okay. I personally took the experience as a wake up call to eliminate the stress and initiate more moments of enthusiasm and relaxation. My doctor said my physical health was just fine, but the stress I'd experienced would only get worse if I did not eliminate the source.

Maybe there are some signs of stress in your life that indicate you need to take a personal analysis.

When was the last time you just took it easy?

Are there stressors taking you further away from a stress-free enthusiastic day?

Are there people in your personal or business life that consistently create a stressful environment for you?

Remember, you are the Captain of the ship. No one can board without your permission. Why not make more choices that reflect enthusiasm rather than stress? The more moments of enthusiasm we experience, the more we experience the spirit in each of us. The opposite prevails in stress- related encounters. We just get further away from the sunshine of everyday.

My notes on enthusiasm:

My personal plan:

CAN YOU STAND THE RAIN?

The good times are fine, they keep a smile
on your face.

But the question is this:

Can You Stand the Rain?

There is a lot of truth to the statement

"No Pain, No Gain."

Everyone loves the comfort zone.

No one wants to deal with the stress when
something goes wrong.

There is a price to pay to keep it sunny
each day.

Are you willing to pay it?

The GG Factor
Can You Stand The Rain?

Can you stand the rain? What a great metaphor! The famous R&B group New Edition had a hit record in the 90s with the same title. The chorus simply said the same thing I'm saying now. Sunny days, everybody loves them. But: Can You Stand The Rain? When you've planted your seeds for success and set some realistic goals for your mind, body and spirit, the most difficult thing to do is remain focused and fired up to achieve them. Every obstacle you could imagine is just waiting to bring the rain down. Well just remember this, every time the rain falls on Mother Earth the grass grows. You and I can't allow blurred vision to causes a perception of life that only reflects problems when all that is happening is a moment of growth challenging us to continue feeding the seeds to success.

"No Pain, No Gain." Betty Wright, a successful singer from Miami is very famous for her message-related hit songs, had a hit with the same title about love.

Sometimes you just got to go through some pain to gain love's reward for patience and perseverance. When I entered graduate school in 1991, I had more rain and pain coming down than you could ever imagine.

Working full time as a musician six nights a week, working as a substitute teacher three to five days a week, raising Jonathan who was only one year old and attending classes from eight to five every Saturday.

There were times when I just wanted to quit!

The rain and the pain were creating a stress that was almost an insurmountable test. But I saw the light at the end. I kept the focus! I knew this too would eventually come to an end. Even after I graduated and had to take twenty more hours of classes and pass some grueling state exams to get teacher certification, I never lost sight of the light at the end of the tunnel. For that, I will always be grateful to Dr. Arlene Sacks, one of my graduate school professors for believing in me when I just wanted to quit. All she said was "you've come to far to turn back now!" Dr. Sacks also simply said, "This too will pass." She and all the beautiful ladies from Barry University were my angels who inspired me to look for the sunshine and to grow from the rain.

My notes on can you stand the rain:

My personal plan:

A WINNER!

You're a winner if you got up today and you have somehow made it through the day.

You're winning if you found the journey along the way is more important than the destination.

You know a winner when he or she speaks only with positive energy to everyone.

A winner knows there's always today to begin again.

A winner lets yesterday be water that has passed under the bridge of life.

A winner knows it is never too late to make the revision to have the vision of a winner!!

The GG Factor
A Winner

We all define winning in our own unique ways. But one thing that's pretty common to all of us is that we all want to win! How many times do you hear news reporters hail the runner-up from the Super Bowl, the NBA championship or the World Series? They don't give the runner up to the New York marathon any of the grand prizes the winner gets even though there may be less than a minute between the 1st and 2nd place times. The winner takes all!! Ask Derek Jeter of the New York Yankees. All he's ever wanted to do is win. He was drafted out of high school and paid $800,000 a year and now makes $20 million a year, having earned four World Series rings and a host of product endorsements.

Winners simply love to win! Isn't it your time?

When my son Jonathan was 10 years old, I coached his optimist basketball team. Most of the kids were beginners. Their parents just wanted their kids to play basketball. They didn't really care about winning. The kids had a different attitude. Even though they weren't that great they knew we kept a score and there was a championship. They also were aware of the fact that every body loves a winner! They wanted to win!

Winning builds self-esteem no matter your age. I would always ask the kids right before a game a simple question. We'd get in the huddle and I'd ask them: "how bad do you want it"? Invariably, they would say: "Real bad coach!!" How bad do you want it?

My notes on a winner

My personal plan:

STRIVE!

STUDY, STUDY, STUDY!

TRY MY VERY BEST TO PASS LIFE'S
TESTS!

RETAIN AND RECALL ALL THAT I CAN!

INNOVATE AND INVENT WITH
POSITIVE   INTENT!

VISUALIZE SUCCESS!

EMPOWER AND EDUCATE   MYSELF
FOREVER!

The GG Factor
STRIVE

Make the acronym STRIVE a daily affirmation
process. Simply put these two words in front of the
word for each letter of the acronym: I WILL!

If you make this a daily routine, you'll always keep your internal
dialogue positive and the universe will accommodate your requests.
Just think if you Study, Try, Retain, Innovate, Visualize and
Empower your mind, body and spirit everyday or as often as you can,
it would be impossible for you not to reach GOALS that will propel
you to the next level in your life.

Imagine walking into your office or classroom feeling like your own
the room! You're on top of the world! You're exhibiting your
optimum physical appearance (OPA). I call it the OPA factor!! The
OPA is a constant. You always want to look good! You know why?
It's simple!! When you look good, you feel good! Think about the
days when you don't think you look good. You don't feel good either!
To each his own when it comes to the OPA. Maybe looking good isn't
important to you.

Maybe you just want to be smart and spiritually grounded. Good for
you, but sooner or later when you not feeling good because of physical
apathy, the imbalance in your life will manifest itself as sickness. You
simply cannot ignore your body! It's your temple. There lies the spirit.

Remember it's all three you see, mind, body and spirit. Balance of the
three is crucial.

STRIVE for it everyday. Live for it in every way. I do! I love it. I
might try a triathlon. I'm 68! Come on just STRIVE for it. It's a lot
closer than you think!!

63

My notes on strive:

My personal plan:

Thoughts after completion of the Disney Marathon 2020

Thanks to Dr. Markson at Markson Chiropractic. You believed I could finish this marathon against all odds.

"WE MUST CONTINUE TO STRIVE NO MATTER WHAT CIRCUMSTANCES WE FACE!"
"NEVER QUIT!"

THOUGHTS

We are what we think about ourselves. Every physical action has been thought about internally long before it becomes an external exhibition.

It's very important to keep thoughts positive. Remember it's still a choice to get back what you give to the universe.

Positive thoughts generate positive feedback and good vibrations from most situations. How are you vibrating? How have your thoughts been lately?

Negatives are only obscure distractions from the main attraction — the positive, the absolute good in life.

The GG Factor
Thoughts

As a teacher, coach/athlete, entertainer, speaker, entrepreneur and a parent. I'm constantly faced with random situations that demand quick, firm decisions.

If my internal dialogue is full of negative energy and gives voice to possible pessimistic outcomes, then the frequency of occurrences in my world would be perceived from a field of constant chaos.

How many times have you had a bad feeling about a situation only to have it manifest itself in your life just the way you'd thought about it. I'm certainly sure that you could have dismissed the negative thoughts and focused on the positive possibilities instead. I started to run marathons at age 43 when I also became a girls cross-country coach at Flanagan High in 1996.

Long before I decided to approach the boys cross country coach to ask if he needed an assistant with over 30 boys and girls, I had negative internal dialogues to talk myself out of the possibility of coaching or running a marathon, being that I was over 40 years old and had a four-year-old son to raise. It wasn't until my thoughts were focused on the positive possibilities and benefits of running everyday with the girls and concurrently training for the Walt Disney Marathon was I able to step out on faith and keep my thoughts full of nothing but absolute good about my decision. Here I am ten years later still running marathons after coaching for seven years and seeing my son Jonathan come to Flanagan and run cross country. Just my thoughts alone could have changed it all!! Here I am 25 years later. I've completed 25 marathons and my son, Jonathan and his wife, Adriana complete the Miami marathon.

My notes on thoughts:

My personal plan:

Cross Country 1996
Flanagan High
Head Coach

HEAD COACH:
Cross Country:
Flanagan High 2000

My son Jonathan
and his wife
Adriana after
completion of the
Miami
Marathon.
Jonathan ran
cross country at
Flanagan High

**Reflecting on the 2020 Disney
Marathon finish. My last
marathon just before COVID-19**

My birthday on November 4, 2019

RELATIONSHIPS

Why do we have to make the road we travel so much more difficult than it has to be?

Who are the people you call your friends?

Are you trying to get in where you don't fit in?

Relationships are like a pair of shoes.

If you force your feet into a pair of shoes that don't fit, you'll surely feel the pain later.

Relationships are no different!

The GG Factor
Relationships

We've all been there and done that when it comes to making a decision to let in the visitor at the door of life. Sometimes we just don't take a good look before we get hooked! Be careful about the who, what, when, where and why before letting someone into your life.

I'm going to let you know that you never get back that which is given from the heart. I know it's easier said than done, but remember that we're all very fragile when it comes to matters of the heart. For in the heart is where the spirit of the source lives. I started to discover that my heart was fragile very early in life.

Decided to let someone in too far too soon! When she decided it was time to move on and let me go I thought I'd never love anyone that way any more. I was only sixteen and Veronica was the junior class queen. So I felt like a king for a while until the queen decided to dismiss the king for another guy. I learned that nothing or no one should ever have that much control over me and my emotional state of mind.

It took some time but I got over Veronica. The relationship captured my mind, body and spirit at a very early age. It's scary how another can become so dominant from the mind, body and spiritual perspectives when initially you think they are in you life only physically; this is especially true when you're very young. Even if the relationship shoes fit very well, be careful and remember that the heart is very fragile.

My own personal experiences have taught me a lot. I'm still learning! You never know it all. You just try to arm the body, mind and spirit from experience with enough to deal with it all! Yes we fall down, but we can always get up and get back in the relationship game.

My notes on relationships:

My personal plan:

Me & my wife Miriam
West Broward High Prom 2023

Disney Marathon

**Gregory &
Miriam Griffith**

Honeymoon Day!

My Sons: Jonathan Griffith & Greg Jr.

Jonathan & Greg

Greg & Greg Jr.

Jonathan's Wedding

Our Wedding Day at Mount Olive Baptist Church: Jonathan Griffith; Angela Griffith; Alyssa Griffith; Miriam Griffith; Gregory Griffith, Sr.; Gregory Griffith, Jr.

My Mother, Big Brother and Sisters
Mom - Essie Mae Griffith
Brother - Nelson Griffith
Sister - Ruby Baker
Sister - Linda Baker

My dad, William H. Hammond and my sons,
Jonathan and Gregory Griffith Jr.
Jonathan's High School graduation

**My sister,
Ruby.**

**My sister,
Linda.**

Graduation day at the University of Central Florida (UCF): My wife Miriam, niece Leontine & my sister Ruby, Leontine's mother

My nieces. Ophelia and Abigail & my sister Pansy Griffith with her 2 daughters.

My nieces, Lauren White, Leontine Morgan & Ruby Baker

My sister Linda and her daughter Lauren.

My dad, William Hammond, my son Gregory Griffith
Jr. and my granddaughter Alyssa Griffith.

Me & my granddaughter,
Alyssa Griffith

Gregory, Miriam, Leontine and
Ruby. Mount Olive Baptist Church

**My sister Linda on my
65th birthday at the
Hollywood Beach.**

**Me and my son, Jonathan G.
Griffith, his wife Adriana
and my wife Miriam.**

My wife Miriam, me & Alyssa.

Greg Jr., Angie, Alyssa

Greg, Angie, Alyssa, Rev. Roundtree & Greg. Jr
Mount Zion Baptist Church, Tampa, Fl.
I was baptized at Mount Zion

Jonathan Griffith graduation from University of Central Florida with Gregory and Greg, Jr.

ARE YOU HAPPY…

…WITH WHO YOU ARE?

…WITH WHERE YOU ARE?

…WITH YOUR LIFE?

Are you looking for someone to make you happy in your external world?

When you start to feel good about yourself from the inside, you will find the place where true happiness starts.

Take the time to ease your mind.

Relax and let go of the external madness. It's a false equation! In other words, it all becomes history quickly.

The GG Factor
Are You Happy

When a student would come to me about a conflict with a peer I'd simply say:

"They can't get in unless you let them!" Your internal dialogue with me, myself and I is where it begins and ends. The visitor at the door of your heart is not always a welcomed one.

I don't know how many times I've just left myself open for the kill, verbally, by an unwanted visitor. The external world has many dimensions and we're all vulnerable to them to some extent, but we always have choices if we be still and recognize that the conflict does not become internal until we engage in the activity, be it mental or physical. We're all faced with random shots from our jobs and personal lives. It's truly a very selfish society we live in. Everyday we get up and bring our attitudes to the concrete jungle and just try to fit in the mix of this thing call life.

Doesn't it make a lot of sense to arm yourself with a positive attitude that everyday is a new beginning, to take the time to be still and be empowered from the inside, to get fired up and be happy from your source that's always there as an constant stream of positive "I can win" energy? You see, your perception is so powerful it takes the picture, sends the message and waits for your external reaction. This is usually the case when things are not going the way we want them to. We engage in a horrible internal dialogue of "oh no, why me" moments that drags us further into the dark room of despair.

I remember failing the state teacher certification exam. I was so upset with the world. I scored a 293. All I needed was a 295! Just one more right answer!! I lost it right there in the computer room when my score came up. The testing room monitor thought I was crazy. All I could think about was the bad, the negative score of 293! I fell very deeply into the dark room of despair. I wavered between questioning my ability to pass the test and wondering if someone was out to get me. You see, my perception was so badly blurred that all I could perceive was the negative from the external. My happiness was totally consumed by the dark cloud of negative thoughts. But you see when I realized I had made a great score and I was much closer than farther away from the goal, the next level in life, my paradigm shifted in the right direction. The rest is history! That was in 1994! I'm happy with my life now! Are you?

My notes on are you happy:

My personal plan:

Fear vs. Faith!

Your worst enemy to success is FEAR!!

In order to be a peak performer under pressure, you must learn to feel the fear and believe that you can still get the job accomplished anyway.

To believe is to have FAITH.

DO IT! N.O.W.
(Remember: No Other Way!)

THE GG FACTOR
Fear vs Faith

How many times will the FEAR monster win? You know the monster in every thought that sends a resounding, negative, pessimistic message of failure if you try to accomplish anything that takes you out of your comfort zone. It's normal to feel uncomfortable about the unknown, but faith is the belief in that which is not seen. Where's your faith? There's a place in a challenge that's never seen until you step out of the box with FAITH, out of the comfort zone!

I remember so vividly, the first time I went to the high diving board at the community swimming pool.

Although I'd been swimming for some time and I'd gone on the lower diving board to jump and dive countless times, there was something about the high diving board that kept the monster on my back. I knew the day was coming because I wanted to experience the feeling of just jumping from the high diving board. Diving was another world! On one occasion at the swimming pool, my big brother was there and asked if I was ready for the challenge. I said a positive, very optimistic YES! He walked with me to the high diving board and simply said, DO IT NOW! I began to climb the ladder to the top and my little heart was thumping louder and harder with each step I took. When I got to the top, I paused for a moment and stepped onto the board and walked to the end, looked and turned around! The monster was winning! I went back to the steps to come down, but all the other kids were there waiting to dive and so was my brother saying, DO IT NOW Gregory! Where's your FAITH?

So I went back to the end of the board and stood there for about 30 seconds. It felt like forever. I said to myself, I can, I can and I did jump. It wasn't very long after that experience that I took my first dive without my brother being there.

Are you at the high diving board of life? How many times are you going to climb the ladder and turn around? How many times are you going to let the fear monster win in the game of life? I've been there more times than you could ever imagine, from my childhood to the day I decided to write this book. I refuse to let the monster win. I choose FAITH, my closest friend!

My notes on fear vs. Faith:

My personal plan:

Greatness!

When you know only your absolute best
will pass the test, this is when greatness
will manifest!

The road to greatness may be long and
lonely,

But the rewards are only for a chosen few!

Who knows? The next great one could be
YOU.

Forget about the destination…Just endure
the journey.

When you finally arrive, you will find the
place for the next great one!

The GG Factor
Greatness

D o you really know how many times Walt Disney went bankrupt before the Magic Kingdom became the most successful tourist attraction in the world?

Did you know that Michael Jordan didn't make his high school basketball team the first time he tried out?

Do you know how many times he took the last shot and missed to win a game?

Do you really think the Wright brothers took flight on the first try?

The universe is just waiting on the next great one. Come on! Get busy! Maybe, just maybe you're next! Who knows what the future holds? All you can do it reach for it with a positive "I can win and find my greatness in the process" attitude.

Are you willing to pay the price for GREATNESS?

I'm a professional entertainer. I make a decent living singing and playing bass guitar in the top clubs in South Florida. This is my 40th year in the industry. I started playing in night clubs when I was only sixteen. My brother, Nelson and sister, Pansy were my managers. We had a lead singer who was only 12 years old. She's my sister, Ruby, the great one! You see Ruby discovered her greatness at a very early age and began to enjoy the journey and keep her eye on the destination, SUCCESS! Of all the jobs and opportunities, she had, nothing has ever taken her away from the greatness that is her voice. You see Ruby is a classic; one of the chosen ones who has the innate gift to sing. Her tag on her car reads: BORN TO SING! Ruby always feels she missed something by not going to college. I just remind her that the great ones have something far more important than all the degrees in the world, a gift from GOD to give to the world! I thank my Mom for God's great gift to this world, her baby girl, Ruby! Here's to you Ruby because we love you! You are the next Great one!

My notes on greatness:

My plan:

Ruby and Greg performing at the Lighthouse Pointe Yacht Club

My sister Ruby Baker. The great one! Born to sing! Debut CD release party.

Ruby live performance on Ft. Lauderdale Beach, Fl.

LIMITATIONS

It is not what you have that counts, it is
what you do
With what you've got!

The only limitations that exist are the ones
you place upon yourself.

If you say "I can't" there is not a chance
for you to win.

But if you say "I can," then it's a sure shot
that you'll give it all you've got to WIN!!!

Think about it! You are what you think of
yourself
Regardless of what anyone else thinks or
says.

The GG Factor
Limitations

Come on! Get out of the box! Your comfort zone is the reason you can't fly! There is truly no limitation to reaching your maximum potential.

Try saying "I can" enough to get tough. Yes, I know the road is going to be rough, but that's not an excuse to just give up. What appears to be going wrong is just a moment of growth.

As the world-famous rapper entrepreneur, Master P would say: There's No limit! Master P had a vision when all he appeared to be faced with was an environment that gave him no reason for living. Against all the odds he was determined to be a successful athlete and businessman. Not only did he form his own record label "No Limit" and become one of the most successful rappers of the decade, he also realized his dream to play professional basketball. He refused to accept limitations. He simply said "I can! I will!" Master P produced his son as a rapper. Both are now doing movies and Master P is a very wealthy and successful entrepreneur simply because he refused to accept labels and limitations.

Have you placed limitations upon yourself because of your environment, race, socio- economic situation or disability? I personally know that it's difficult to have a vision when all that appears to be is darkness. The odds just don't seem to be favorable, but Reverend Joel Osteen speaks about God's favor in his incredible book, "Your Best Life Now!" If you claim it in the spirit it will manifest itself in your physical world. Just start by simply saying "I can! I will! I have to win and there are no limitations!!" You have God's favor!

My notes on limitations:

My personal plan:

BELIEVE IN YOURSELF!

If you do not believe in yourself why would you expect anyone else to believe in you?

You are one of a kind.

Everyone has a light under the sun.

Let yours shine brightly!

The GG Factor
Believe in Yourself

The light only becomes unseen when you stop or never start believing. You see, it never stops shining. The moment you discover the source, the light comes on in your life. It's only incognito because you've lost or never found that it's just waiting to be discovered. Seek and you'll always find that the light is waiting to shine in every area of your life. Mind, body and spirit work like the parts of a car. When the car is tuned up and all the parts are working in complete balance you get a start from the ignition that sends a signal to the car that's a mission to move.

Just think if the battery was weak, a tire was too low on air or there wasn't enough oil in the engine to get it to go? A breakdown in communication causes stagnation. Once the car is repaired it's able to move on. Do you really think your life is any different? Remember, you must first believe in yourself. Your thoughts are like the key to the ignition of a mind with a strong battery. You got to get FIRED UP and stay FOCUSED about your MIND, BODY, and SPIRIT! The analogy is real here if you'll just BELIEVE.

Cars now have computers to send reminders when imbalance occurs with a warning to get service or risk a breakdown. We get signals in life from the source. It's an intuitive reminder that something isn't right. Listen to your intuition! Believe in yourself. It's the fuel in the faith tank that keeps your light shining forever.

Unfavorable circumstances have a way of pulling us into the dark tunnel of despair. The further we fall the darker and deeper the tunnel gets. You lose a job, a relationship goes bad, your health starts to fail or you just lose a battle with life's multiplicity of challenging calls. You can run if you'd like, but you cannot hide from life's challenging rides. They're all part of the journey. That believing in yourself when they occur will only make you stronger.

When I was sleeping on the floor and taking a bath in the back yard under a hose hanging from a tree in Liberty City, in the heart of a rough area of Miami in 1981, I had a very low fuel tank of faith. All I could see and feel was life not being fair to me. I had no money, no job, and I was having a hard time trying to keep the light on to make it through it all. But you see I never stop believing that this too will pass and my mission to be a successful musician would let my light shine at last. I wasn't alone. There were seven of us trying to make it and many of the days were very, very long. But one day someone I'd met along the way sent me a gift that showed up in an unexpected way--a leather jacket; some money and a small bible with a letter that I still have to this day as a reminder that the source is guiding my everyday. I eventually recorded an album moved on in my life to be proud to say I survived the challenge to see the light. I never stopped believing. When you just BELIEVE against all the odds is when the source's light shines through it all. NEVER STOP BELIEVING IN YOURSELF!!

My notes on believe in yourself:

My personal plan:

Be Optimistic!

Be truly optimistic! It's the ultimate step to a foundation for success in life!

Optimism defeats any opportunity for thoughts of lack and limitation to create negative, pessimistic, stagnating energy.

Optimistic people always have a vision of light shining at the end of the tunnel as a reminder that nothing can stop them from reaching the next level.

Energize your thoughts with powerful optimism.

Be patient. Stay in active pursuit.

Be optimistic for a successful outcome!

It's always closer than you think!

The GG Factor
Be Optimistic

When you hear the stories of successful people, they may be very different in origin and diverse in each endeavor, but there's one thing that's universal: They're always optimistic no matter what the circumstances. They stay in the game. An optimist will never lose site of the light at the end.

No one knew what the challenges may have been for professional actors and singers like Jim Carey, Jennifer Lopez, Britney Spears, R. Kelly, Keenan Ivory Wayans, Halle Berry, Chris Rock, Eddie Murphy, Madonna, Whitney Houston, Queen Latifah, Donny

Mc Clurkin, Beyonce or Fantasia. I've personally seen them on television or heard them speak on radio about their struggle. All of them just refuse to quit. It wasn't an option.

When I made a very serious decision to pursue a career in the music industry in June 1976, I had just gotten my degree in business administration from Florida A & M University. I'd been playing bass guitar in bands since I was 16 and I loved it. I packed everything I owned and got on the back of a U-Haul truck and went to Newark, New Jersey to pursue a recording deal for my band.

Believe it or not I had a record contract six months later against every odd you could imagine. You see, we refused to quit and the universe just seem to answer the call. After being with my band for well over a decade, I decided to leave, get married and start a new life in Miami. Against all the odds over 20 years later, I'm still doing what I like to do. I play my bass and sing for a living only because I've always remained optimistic and refuse to quit.

I remember coming home from one of my performances and watching a late night infomercial from Carlton Sheets on how to get into real estate with no money down. One night I decided to buy the money back program and try my luck. I procrastinated for months before I finally made a firm optimistic commitment to dive in and go the distance. In one year I not only bought a $300,000 apartment building, I also bought a duplex with less than $3,000. All the investments happen with (OPM): Other Peoples Money. I will not tell you it was easy, because it wasn't. But I will tell you it wasn't impossible because I was optimistic and persistent in my belief. I'm still in the game.

106

I refuse to quit!
Be optimistic! It works if you work it!

My notes on be optimistic:

My personal plan:

RESPECT

How do you expect me to respect you if you don't respect yourself?

Give respect to get respect.
Speak to others the way you'd want them to speak to you.

Be patient with the old and the dependent, for one day you will be old and dependent too!

When you think about it, no one is truly independent.

Your greatest contributions to life are also the beginning of your greatest blessings.

Think about it?

GIVE RESPECT TO GET RESPECT!

The GG Factor
Respect

Aretha Franklin made r-e-s-p-e-c-t an anthem for all of us! But, for a very long time we've had extremely different perspectives on the basic premise of respect in this country. From Brown vs. The Board of Education to the right to vote, we've come along way baby! Living in Miami, you get the real deal when the fight for freedom becomes blurred by the lack of respect for humanity.

The Haitians and the Cubans are refugees trying to make it to freedom, but the respect given to either race is so biased that we've just blatantly ignored the rights of one race while favoring another. Why do we just ignore the rights because we have the position or is it just lack of respect? Our country's border control has used some extremely aggressive measures to stop illegal aliens. We lost at sea an innocent six year old who was seeking freedom to find respect he couldn't get in Cuba. He died only because someone with position and authority with no respect for the rights of another to live did what ever they had to do by any means necessary. Does it make it right even if the action meant disrespect to the point of death?

Do you remember what we did to another little Cuban boy who made it here but our government said "I don't think so, you got to go?" Wow, talking about lack of respect! Do you really think one more kid could destroy this country or be the next Derek Jeter? When does the madness subside? Respect seems so hard to get when someone else just refuses to give it back. Is it that hard to see that freedom is only a few feet away? Did we just forget how far they've come to get a little respect to live?

From a relationship perspective, domestic violence is one our country's leading causes of death! Physical and mental abuse are out of control. No respect for the right to agree to disagree. One human being just decides to be in control of another's body, mind, and soul.

Our relationships are the origins of either a healthy environment to thrive or a quest by someone to take another's pride and respect. Just a reminder, give respect first to get respect.

It's never too late! Ask Nelson Mandela. How long did he wait? How much did he take?

My notes on respect

My personal plan:

FOCUS, FOCUS, FOCUS

It's very easy to stray off the course and get blurred vision.

Distractions are the obstacles that pull you away from the sunshine of every day.

Reaction from your perception creates the paradigm in your mind.

What you see is what you get!!

Focus on nothing but the positive and the good, and then the vision is understood.

Don't let fear in! That's when blurred negative vision wins!

Stay Fired Up! Stay Focused!

The GG Factor
Focus

Be it body, mind or spirit, focus is the foundation for success. I didn't run my first marathon until I was 43. It wasn't until I decided to get fired up and focused, honor the commitment and stop letting the fear of failure win, that I was able to start my training. I distinctly remember when I could barely run a mile. But, because I was determined to honor the commitment, I remained focused. One mile eventually became easy. Then five miles became easy until I was running 10k meets and continuing to increase the mileage. I started running at least two marathons a year in 1997. I really got hooked and FOCUSED!

Even as a professional musician, it was very easy for me to lose the focus and get blurred vision from my negative perception. When I came to Miami to start my production company and work the nightclub scene, I faced elements of the business that didn't surface until I decided to become a band leader and a lead vocalist.

Racism in the south was a given but for the most part remained a hush, hush subject. My first band was a seven piece show and dance band. The majority of the players were black. Every time I went to a club to play the manager always approached the white guitar player and just assumed he was the leader. I was pretty tolerant with this pattern initially, but the frequency of occurrence blurred my vision. All I began to perceive was negative, negative, negative! The fear monster was winning! I actually wanted to quit the music business. After a year of this madness a funny thing happened. I reduced my band size to five pieces. The only Blacks were the female singer and I. I went from struggling to get jobs to having a full year of contracts and a brand new BMW. When the band was reduced I had the challenge of becoming the prominent male vocalist.

Remember, I'm the leader but I'm the bass guitar player and sound tech. I was not a singer! I struggled with musicians that couldn't sing until I took some vocal lessons and just said that I can do this. All I needed was the vote of confidence from my vocal coach. She simply said: "Gregory, stay focused and believe in yourself"!

I've completed 25 marathons, singing and performing over 40 years later.

I know there's something that you've wanted to get focused about that you're running from. You're just letting fear win. You've got blurred vision.

Now is the time to get fired up and get focused! It's your time! What's your perception doing to the possibilities? They're just waiting for you to go the distance.

My notes on focus, focus, focus:

My personal plan:

It's Not Easy

No one has ever said that life is supposed
to be easy.
So don't be so hard on yourself.

If a challenge in life seems to be too much
to handle, it's that way for a reason.

Experience is the road to growth. Just
remember there are no rules to what
road you choose, and you don't get a
map to show you which way to go.

But, you've got to make decisions based on
your own personal life experiences. All
choices have consequences that can impact
our lives forever!

The GG Factor
It's Not Easy

How many of life's experiences can you recall that weren't a challenge to your comfort zone at all? When things are easy and very predictable, we just go with the flow. No need to stress. No need to pass a test. But when we need to step out of the box and deal with a test it becomes hard to even find the time to rest. You see it's in the moments of the challenge that we become more focused and monitor what's happening. These are the times of uncertainty to grow in ways that we thought we didn't know, but you've got to remember that you're the captain of the ship, the star of your show.

When I decided to become a teacher, I knew that it wouldn't be easy. I had been out of college for over 15 years and working as a full time musician had nothing to do with teaching. I was very reluctant to make the commitment because I knew that I would have to make school my ultimate priority even if I was a new daddy and working five nights a week as an entertainer. I had to take my son to a sitter and practice with my band and find the time to study and still be my wife's man. Yes it was an act that a lot of times I didn't get right. But who said it would be easy when you want to qualify yourself for a chance to advance to get a bigger paycheck and meet life's demands. Now that I look back and have the time to reflect I must admit that I'm glad I made a decision to step out of the box. Now I have something called credentials to knock on the doors that could open opportunities that at one time in my life I would've never thought of. If they made it easy to grow in life no one would probably make the sacrifice. We'd all just stay in the box.

My notes on it's not easy:

My personal plan:

LOVE YOURSELF!
LOVE LIFE!

It's far more important to have a high level
of self-esteem than it is to have a high I.Q.

Love Yourself!
Love Life!

The world needs your contribution.

Unique is what you'll always be,

So
Don't be afraid to let your inner light shine
brightly.

The GG Factor
Love Yourself, Love Life

L ove Yourself!

It's truly up to you! It's your choice! Life isn't always fair, but that's not an excuse for you to not feel good about yourself. I know it's important for every student to make the best grades they can in school and I'm sure every parent would love to see their kid go to college, but every kid in college doesn't have the IQ of a genius. Every student isn't college material. One thing that every student of life has to have regardless of the level of IQ is a high level of self-esteem. When you feel good about yourself the universe brings you all the good you're seeking. It's just the opposite when you're feeling bad, negative and predicting the worst that could happen. You can bank on it; the worst is just waiting to validate your negative thoughts. Our thoughts are just like wavelengths. We're all vibrating on frequencies mentally. How many times have you said to yourself, "I don't have a good vibe about something or someone? You usually follow your instincts. When you ignore them and the outcome of a situation manifests around the thoughts you had you should know how powerful your feelings are. Be still and become empowered by your thoughts.

I start everyday with meditation to empower my spirit with positive affirmations to keep my energy positive regardless to whom I meet in the course of the day that may bring negative energy my way. I affirm that there is only absolute good in my world. Every encounter that alters that is just a false equation. It's their problem in their world. Think about it. Nothing is permanent unless you internalize and process it. Why process nothing but good thoughts. They make you feel good. Bad thoughts just make you feel bad.

Good thoughts, high self-esteem! Bad thoughts, low and no self-esteem!

Case studies conducted on babies who are given nothing but love and unconditional loving, nurturing thoughts by nurses, concurrent with babies who weren't nurtured and were rarely spoken to or given loving moments revealed that nearly all the nurtured babies cried a lot less, weren't sick and almost always were smiling and active. The other babies cried constantly, had medical concerns and didn't appear to be happy.

It makes you wonder and think---if words can cut like a knife or be as soothing as a morning breeze even to an infant who just wants to be pleased, imagine what they do for us as adults in our times of need. Self-esteem is priceless. It's developed from every encounter we have, good or bad, happy or sad. Take in the good and try your best to ignore the rest. It's another one of life's toughest test.

My notes on love yourself, love life:

My personal plan:

Time and Space

Time and space will never erase what life's experiences teach us.

To really enjoy all that life has to offer is the only way to maximize everyday.

Even when the days seem long and things appear to have gone wrong, there's always something good to take from the experience to make you strong.

So when the sun doesn't shine and the rain starts to fall, just remember to stay positive through it all.

The sun will shine again my friend!

The GG Factor
Time and Space

Every encounter from the external is no coincidence. Your perception determines the reception. Don't be so quick to draw premature conclusions. You're only creating a negative illusion. You see then, life just becomes very confusing. Time and space are not illusions. They're real! Take your time about life's matters of the heart. The space is your environment. It play's a crucial part to finding life's place of balance.

Be careful. Be selective. Don't forget. You're still captain of the ship.

I'm absolutely sure you can recall incidents from your past that have affected where you are in the present. We hear about the traumatic incidents that become the heavy luggage of life's time and space from many people on talk shows, in magazines and newspaper articles, on the daily news, in movies and as public speakers. The sad reality is our encounters have their etiologies from very early in our lives. Physical and mental abuse from parents or a spouse is very hard to erase. We don't forget but we should reflect and grow. It's time to check that luggage. Take it out of your life. Time and space don't discriminate. Waste your time, waste your space. If you keep the luggage it will only get very heavy along the way. When do we empty the luggage of negative time and space?

A procrastinator knows there's an agenda. It's not until life's frustration and fears have become so dominant that he will then prioritize the moment. It's usually at this point in life that the agony of defeat has won.

Don't be time and space's next victim. Life is just too short in the physical. As we grow in stature we start to move so fast that we lose sight of things that matter a whole lot more than anything in the physical, material world, our spirit. You see in spirit there's only maturity. Our job in the physical is to occupy our time and space to grow spiritually. That's why I asked you the question: Are you in touch with the source? Moving too fast in time and space will get you blurred from the source.

Slow down! Get the mix right. It's your time and space!

My notes on time and space:

.

My personal plan:

HARMONY

When a marching band plays a song all
the parts are heard as one. Arrangement
of notes creates chords of harmony to be
enjoyed by anyone.

Music is a universal language that any
culture can understand with their eyes and
ears in any land.

Even if a musician cannot read, he can still
hear the harmony, indeed, and play a part
that pleases.

A singer can find the part that needs to be
sung even if she can't see the harmony
chord that's written for everyone.

As long as there's an ear to listen and the
right chord is played the universal
language of harmony is made.

We have the opportunity to live in
complete harmony with one another. Our
universal chords start with a smile rather

than a frown for both are acceptable by
anyone that's around.

But when a chord has a bad note the sound
is not pleasing because like a frown it's
unwanted for a reason.

Try to keep harmony in your life by
beginning each day with a smile, the
universal language understood by all
across the globe through every traveled
mile!

The GG Factor
Harmony

When I was sixteen my brother formed my first band. I was the bass player in a seven-piece band called the Mighty Good and Strong. We barely knew a handful of songs but we knew when a harmony was wrong. When things are wrong musically you just know it if you got the ears. I had been in marching bands since I was thirteen. I played trumpet. We all were in our high school's band, so we had some training and decent ears. We were attempting to learn songs from the record to play in talent shows and in the local night clubs. We practiced nearly every day after school in the band room. I vividly remember some of our biggest arguments occurring because of the vocal harmony or musical chords in the songs we were learning. Remember we were very young and no one person knew a lot more than the next guy.

So we'd finally agree even if it wasn't always the best harmony. But one day we went to look for some amplifiers for our guitars and vocals and we met these two guys who were twins. Their names were Richard, a guitarist, and Ralph a keyboardist. They were our ages but you'd think they were adult professionals. Boy, could they play! Richard could make a cheap guitar sound like a classic Fender stratocaster played by Jimi Hendrix , one of the greatest rock guitarists of all time. The day we heard Richard play we smiled at each other and just knew we were witnessing harmony and musical chemistry. The universal language of the ears and eyes of music were connected. Richard came to a rehearsal and joined our band! A white guy playing with seven black kids in the 70s, this rarely happened, but we had innate harmony. We hit the right chord. After a few rehearsals we were pleading with Richard's parents to let him perform with us and the next thing you knew we were out performing everywhere.

My notes on harmony:

My personal plan:

**The Harmony of my
big band!
Gregory Griffith
Productions**

**My first band in college
1973!**

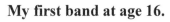

My first band at age 16.

TRAMA! ORIGINAL
RECORDING BAND 1976

T.K. RECORDING ARTIST

TRAMA

FOR INFORMATION CONTACT:
Lawrence Hires   (813) 677-3963
Issac Guest   (813) 677-6329
Gregory Griffith (813) 243-0532
P.O. Box 4618, Tampa, Fla. 3367'

INTEND TO WIN!

If you intend to win in life, then you should be prepared to pay the price.

There is a sacrifice that's worth the price when you look back at positive results that make you feel nice.

When life's challenges seems to keep you down, and you can't seem to see the light at the end of the tunnel, don't ever forget:

Being a winner is one of life's toughest tests.

We're born with the innate ability to survive, to win in life, not just exist.

Make the most of every day.

Begin with the attitude of a winner!

INTEND TO WIN!!

The GG Factor
Intend to Win

When you have a plan, passion or purpose in life in your mind, you intend to win! The sacrifice always involves the tug of war with what is really priority and worthy of giving up to get what you're seeking. If it's success you're seeking you'd better be prepared to pay a big price. You must decide which one is for you and implement your lifestyle management strategy to win.

Security or freedom! Security is nice. You get a job, buy a car, buy a home, establish some credit and maintain a position of secure survival in life through your position for someone's company. If you are content with the parameters to which you can grow and stay secure, then you're set for life until the company or your position changes or is eliminated. Corporate down sizing is an American way of life. It's scary!

The alternative is freedom. Freedom is usually the result of a very heavy sacrifice to be in total control of your destiny and leave a lasting legacy for your family.

I'm working on freedom. You see you can always begin again like I have in the security arena with intent to move on or just dive off the high diving board into the pool and swim for freedom's gate. Some of our greatest success stories have manifest themselves in a dramatic swim to freedom's gate.

I honestly started right off the high diving board as a young college graduate with a business degree and hungry to become an entrepreneur in the music industry. It wasn't until 15 years later that I decided to enter graduate school, leaving the quest for freedom and sought stability for the sake of my younger son. I became a teacher for the security of a job. I don't regret the decision. My son became a gifted student, a good athlete and socially adjusted with his peers. He is grounded with solid foundations for success physically, mentally and spiritually. Still, I feel the high diving board is waiting for me to take another dive.

Have you made sacrifices for family that seemed to stagnate your aspirations for freedom? Maybe you're thinking you're too old or you can't get the money for school. I could list many obvious obstacles that are simply roads to growth if you elect to take the dive from security to freedom. Freedom isn't for everyone.

Security is a good thing. The foundation for any successful business is built on someone's dream becoming reality with a team of security-based employees who facilitate the freedom searcher's strategy for success.

Right now, innovative technology is running the world. Everyday some knew computer guru intends to win with a vision to be the new freedom giant on the tech block. They all usually start from the security block and the creative bug from the source shifts their paradigm to a vision of freedom. You wonder what would be the answer if you asked the CEO of Microsoft, Bill Gates or Dell Computer's CEO Michael Dell which one have they always wanted, security or freedom. I'm certain of this, they INTEND TO WIN!

My notes on intend to win:

My personal plan:

COMMITMENTS

The power of commitment makes all the difference between success and failure.

Focus fuels commitment's tank and the end result is a deposit as real as cash flow in the bank.

Commitments are simply links in the chain to the next level.

Before you can travel commitment's road, you must ask yourself, "do I have the map of my goal locked deep in my soul where the compass of life makes everything alright?"

Make the commitment.

More important: KEEP the commitments!

The GG Factor
Commitments

We all know that it's easier said than done when it comes to commitments. Every obstacle you could imagine is just waiting to make the journey to greatness very difficult. Remember how important focus is to honor the commitment. Don't get blurred vision. When I made a commitment to become a cross country coach for Flanagan High in September 1996. I honored the commitment for seven years. I also made a commitment to run at least one marathon a year as long as I was a coach. I'm training for my 10th marathon now to run in February 2006.

That's one a year for a decade. That's commitment!

Don't think that it wasn't very difficult to honor my commitments to be a responsible father, husband, full time teacher, coach, professional entertainer four nights a week, entrepreneur, and train for the marathon!! I'll be very honest here, I've always been multi tasked and there were times when the walls were closing in from stress, but the exercise kept the stress down and I just loved what I was doing. I stopped coaching to focus more on becoming a speaker, author and entrepreneur.

Time management, diet, exercise, proper rest, spiritual empowerment from your source and strategic goal setting are crucially important to successfully honor your commitments. Every one of your physical, mental and spiritual obligations is an intricate link in your chain to successful commitment implementation.

On the next page you'll find a Personal Empowerment Recognition Program (PERP) commitment pledge that will guide you through the next 30 days. Right before you started the book, I asked you some very important questions about the three important areas of your life to establish a PERP for success.

NOW is the time to take action. Make the commitment. Sign it. Copy it and carry it with you as a reminder to remain FIRED UP and FOCUSED to honor your commitments!! Good Luck! Remember to always have the vision to make the revision to be a WINNER!

My notes on commitments:

My personal plan:

PERSONAL EMPOWERMENT RECOGNITION PROGRAM
(PERP)

30 DAYS TO A NEW YOU COMMITMENT:

I_____will remain FIRED UP and FOCUSED for the next 30 days on my physical, mental and spiritual commitments to establish my PERP for success in my life. I will affirm everyday that I STRIVE to keep my commitment alive.

I am dedicated to adapting a new lifestyle management process for SUCCESS.

Signed_____

Witnessed_____

Date_____

Get a witness that will be a positive reinforcement to honor your PERP commitment for the next 30 days. Have them call to help you stay fired up and focused, or even become a PERP partner with you. You want positive energy and lots of love! At the end of the month, assess your pre and post data. Make another 30-day commitment! I'm going to be the first to say congratulations! You made the commitment. Let the lifestyle change begin and become a permanent transformation. Call me if you need a coach! I'm ready to get you FIRED up!

30 Days to a New You Implementing the Strategies

WEEK 1

Focus on Establishing Foundations for Success in All Three Areas

1. What are your goals for the first week?

Physical _____

_____

Mental _____

_____

Spiritual _____

Suggested Strategies:
*Focus on your motivation.
*Why are you doing this?
*Why is it important to you?
*What do you wish to accomplish in the first few days?
*Talk to your doctor before you start a new regimen.
*Can you achieve your mental goals with your present skills?
*Start a daily log of your diet.
* Clear your pantry and refrigerator of any tempting foods.
*Weigh yourself in the morning right after you get up.
* Begin an exercise plan.
* Drink at least 8 8-ounce glasses of water a day.
*Try 5-10 minutes of silence and positive internal dialogue with your source before you begin each day.
* Keep a positive attitude.

30 Days to a New You Implementing the Strategies

WEEK 2

Focus on Establishing Foundations for Success in All Three Areas

1. What are your goals for the second week?

_____

Physical _____

_____

Mental _____

_____

Spiritual _____

Suggested Strategies:

*Acknowledge any positive changes

*What have been the most noticeable results?

*Have you been able to break bad habits?

*Stay consistent with meal times.

* Increase your exercise routine to at least 30 minutes a day.

* Remember, the bathroom scale doesn't measure success, it monitors only the physical.

* Don't forget you are the winner in this race only if you don't quit.

* Be creative! The genius in you will come shining through.

*Stay fired up about the new you.

*Continue to find time to meditate consistently.

*Regardless of the results, stay positive and in active pursuit of all your goals.

30 Days to a New You Implementing the Strategies

WEEK 3

Focus on Establishing Foundations for Success in All Three Areas

1. What are your goals for the third week?

Physical

Mental

Spiritual

Suggested Strategies:

*Remember, it's still about all of you; physical, mental and spiritual.

*This is the halfway point! It is the glass half empty or half full.

*Focus! Focus! Focus!

*Time is like money! Do not waste it!

*NOW= No Other Way! Who knows what the future holds!

*The only limitations that exist are the ones you place upon yourself. If you say I can, then you'll win!

*Are you monitoring your results?

*You should be empowered from your time alone with your source.

30 Days to a New You Implementing the Strategies

WEEK 4
Focus on Establishing Foundations for Success in All Three Areas

1. What are your goals for the fourth week?

_____

Physical_____

_____

Mental _____

_____

Spiritual

Suggested Strategies:

*Welcome to your new lifestyle. You have arrived!

*What have you learned from this experience?

*Have you found that you have a lot more will power when a goal is in sight?

*Has your attitude changed?

*Do you feel empowered by your achievement?

* Keep the FOCUS! Activate or Stagnate! Keep your life in drive, don't procrastinate!

*Do not forget your strategies implementation!

*You are the most important person in your life! You have to live with yourself.

*When you are hungry, drink water first. If you still feel hungry, have a healthy snack!

*Increase your exercise time.

*Increase your meditation time.

*Can the genius continue to play for another 30 days?

*Sign another 30 Days to New You contract!

*Remember, it's always about the next level.

*Do not forget that you are the "Captain of Your Ship"!

Contact Gregory Griffith *to get your company or school fired up for the next level!*

Activate or Stagnate NOW!

Take the 30-day challenge to empower your team
With the tools necessary to get the maximum potential
from each individual.

Contact me for a great edutainment keynote or workshop to take
your company or school vision to the next level.

Twitter: @Greggriffith1
Instagram: @Gregory_Griffith

Facebook:
Personal: www.facebook.com/gregory.chalina
Production: www.facebook.com/people/Gregory-Griffith-
Productions

YouTube Channel:
Personal: YouTube.com/Gregorytheactivator
Production: YouTube.com/gregorygriffithprod

LinkedIn: Gregory Griffith

Tiktok: @gg72664

Visit my websites at
https://www.theactivator.net
https://www.gregorygriffithproductions.com
and https://gregorygriffithevents.blogspot.com
or call our office at **954-435-3839** to book your next event.

You may write to me at:
Gregory Griffith PO Box 824035
Pembroke Pines, Fl. 33082
Fax: 954-435-4660
Cell: 305-498-2266
Toll free: 833-80-ACTIV
833-802-2848
Email: info@theactivator.net /
info@gregorygriffithproductions.com

Printed in the USA
CPSIA information can be obtained
at www.ICGtesting.com
LVHW050009250124
769490LV00092B/3825